CUSTOMARY LAWS, FEMINISM AND STATUS OF WOMEN IN BODO SOCIETY

RITURAJ BASUMATARY | SWMAOSHAR BRAHMA

Contents

Preface

This book deals with the Customary Laws, Feminism and Status of Women in Bodo Society. Hope that the publication of this book will be useful. This book may not be free from errors and constructive criticisms are welcomed for the improvement of this book.

Abstract

The gender relations of the Bodo tribes which constructs inequality can be analysed looking at the customary law of the tribal communities in India. Customary law is a part of the tribal traditional customs and practices where the tribes considered it 'intrinsic to their identity and culture'. Customary law can be understood as 'an established system of immemorial rules which evolved from the way of life and natural wants of the people, the general context of which was a common knowledge, coupled with precedents applying to special cases, which were retained in the memories of the chief and his counsellors, their sons and their son's son, until forgotten, or until they became part of the immemorial rules'. The operation of customary laws acts as a powerful tool to define the roles of men and women and dictate acceptable standards of behaviour. Bodo women's social and economic status continues to be influenced by customary rules.

Almost all the customary law of the region which includes 'people's beliefs, customs, social mores, percepts, rites and usages practiced since time immemorial, are not always conducive to the interests of women' and the customary laws relating to 'property and marriage are highly oppressive to women.' As have been mentioned above, women in the region shoulder heavy economic responsibilities viz-a-viz men. Yet their customary laws deny them equal rights to property and inheritence which is one of the important factors affecting their empowerment.

The customary law in matters of marriage and divorce also are far from favourable to women. Among many of the tribes in India, women are treated as mere commodities which can be seen in their custom of bride price. Bride price prevails among the various communities in India where the bridegroom has to pay certain amount of money to the girl's parent. This custom of bride price which is practiced among the tribes is based on the recognition of the importance of women's role in the economic sphere. It is the 'reflection of the fact that women are a productive worker in the economy of the tribe'. Though bride price was paid to compensate the girl's family for their loss of an 'economically active member', it has provided man with the 'justification to treat his wife as a disposable commodity.' The payment of bride price did not protect women against exploitation within the family rather it creates limitationon women's right to initiate divorce as it 'entails the obligation to return the bride price to the husband. So women prefer to suffer in silence ever if she is ill treated rather than take resources to divorce'. In most of the communities of India, the customary laws are constituted and interpreted by male alone. Women have no role in decision making. Due to their customary laws, they are not allowed to share their ideas in village decision making. Women are excluded from participating in all the important decision making institutions.

Almost all the communities in India are patrilineal society where descent is traced from father to son except for the state of Meghalaya, where the Khasi and the Garo tribes follow the matrilineal system where descent is traced from mother to the daughter. Yet what remains similar is that patriarchy rules in all these societies as well. Women are never allowed to represent the family or the kin group at the community level. Moreover, they are neither being given any authority at the social level. Thus, even though women have property rights in the matrilineal society, but when it comes to decision making whether it is in matrilineal or patrilineal societies, it is regarded as the domain of men.

Keywords:- Customary, Laws, Feminism, Bodo, Society.

CHAPTER I

Introduction

Geographically, men and women share the same space, but everywhere in the world, women are accorded a lower status than men. The North Eastern region of India has been considered as a backward region in terms of growth in per capita income. However, there is a perception that the status of women is higher in the North Eastern Region of the country in comparison with the status of women in all India average. It is found from the analysis that the status of women in the region is comparatively better than the rest of the country only in some selected indicators. The indicators reveal that women have a very low degree of freedom of movement and low level of control over themselves in the North Eastern Region.

Northeast is better off than the other parts of India as a whole in terms of gender equality. However, inequality between women and men exists in the region inspite of the predominance of various ethnic groups who by and large do not believe in sex discrimination. The study reveals that women are relatively disempowered and enjoy somewhat lower status than that of men in the region. Gender gap exists in terms of access to education, employment and health. A large gender gap exists in political participation both at the levels of state and nation. Among the northeastern states, Meghalaya, Manipur and Mizoram show relatively lesser degree of gender inequality in terms of work participation, literacy, infant mortality and sex ratio. The situation is however adverse in case of Tripura, Assam and Sikkim.

The status of women in India has been a major debate in the Indian society. Since before the independence of the country the women have been the major sufferers. In a patriarchal society women are regarded as the powerless and marginalized section in the Indian society. The condition of women deteriorated in the post Vedic period due to the influence of Vedic literature like "smriti ", "sutra", "purana". It was regarded by the founder of "Smriti" Manu that women should be under the male member of the house, during her childhood she would be under control of her father , under her husband during her youth and her son during old age. The social evil practice such as purdah system, child marriage, sati etc started prevailing in the society which led to the decline of the position of women in the Indian society. The oppression against women was led to the clash between class and caste. The lower caste women were sexually discriminated by the higher caste.

CHAPTER II

Literature Review

The status of women improved after the Bhakti movement.In 18th century several attempt were made by the social reformers like Raja Rammohan Roy, Swami Dayanand Saraswati, Mahadev Govind Ranande, Anee Besant etc. to abolish social evil practice like sati, child marriage etc. After independence various legislations such as Special marriage act 1954, Hindu Marriage act 1956, and the anti Dowry act 1961 were passed to improve the position of women. The constitution of India also guarantees Right to Equality. Whereas living in a male dominated society women had to forgo some rights she acquires. Despite of the several attempts made by the reformers and the government the status of women has not yet improved the rising incidents against women. The prevailing social practices such as age-old institution of prostitution, 'devadasi' system, rape, sexual harassment at workplace and domestic violence etc. are also the primary reason.

According to the World Bank report, is the major cause of female infertility. The presence of excessive malnutrition among female children as compared to male children is basically due to differences in the intra family allocation of food between the male and female children. Normally, the male members are fed before the female members of the family. According to Human Development Report, in rural Punjab, 21% of girls in low income families suffer from severe malnutrition as compared with 3 % of boys in the same family. Even the low income boys are far better than upper income girls. Girl babies are less breast fed than boy babies. 60% of girl babies are born with low birth weight. Sometimes due to economic distress and natural calamities like floods, droughts or earthquakes, the discrimination against the female child increases. Moreover it has been confirmed by various studies that the girl's diet is inferior to the boy's diet both in quality and quantity. Boys are given more nutritive foods like milk, eggs, butter, ghee, fruits, and vegetables as compared to girls. Due to this inferior quality diet, girls are more vulnerable to infections and diseases. The reason again is that families spend less on medication for girls than for boys.

CHAPTER III

Customary Laws

The customary law in matters of marriage and divorce also are far from favourable to women. Among many of the tribes in India, women are treated as mere commodities which can be seen in their custom of bride price. Bride price prevails among the various communities in India where the bridegroom has to pay certain amount of money to the girl's parent. This custom of bride price which is practiced among the tribes is based on the recognition of the importance of women's role in the economic sphere. It is the 'reflection of the fact that women are a productive worker in the economy of the tribe'. Though bride price was paid to compensate the girl's family for their loss of an 'economically active member', it has provided man with the 'justification to treat his wife as a disposable commodity.' The payment of bride price did not protect women against exploitation within the family rather it creates limitation on women's right to initiate divorce as it 'entails the obligation to return the bride price to the husband. So women prefer to suffer in silence ever if she is ill treated rather than take resources to divorce'. In most of the communities of India, the customary laws are constituted and interpreted by male alone. Women have no role in decision making. Due to their customary laws, they are not allowed to share their ideas in village decision making. Women are excluded from participating in all the important decision making institutions.

Almost all the communities in India are patrilineal society where descent is traced from father to son except for the state of Meghalaya, where the Khasiand the Garo tribes follow the matrilineal system where descent is traced from mother to the daughter. Yet what remains similar is that patriarchy rules in all these societies. Women are never allowed to represent the family or the kin group at the community level. Moreover, they are neither being given any authority at the social level. Thus, even though women have property rights in the matrilineal society, but when it comes to decision making whether it is in matrilineal or patrilineal societies, it is regarded as the domain of men.

The social exclusion of women is also a major issue in the Indian society. The term "social exclusion" was originally coined by Rene Lenoir in 1974, the French Social Action Secretary of State in the Chirac government referring to various social categories of people, such as the mentally and physically handicapped, single parents, substance users and other groups unprotected by social insurance. The gender discrimination is one of the major issues in Indian society. The social exclusion of women has been an historic phenomenon.

CHAPTER IV

Feminism in Bodo Society

The Bodos are one of the Indigenous People of the present day Assam and the other neighbouring states of North East India. At a certain period of time in history, the Bodos have been ruling the different parts of North East India under different Bodo Kings and Queens under different dynasties. Most of the places on the banks of Brahmaputra river were inhabited by the Bodos. The Bodo society is a patriarchical society. So father is considered to be the head of the family in a Bodo society. But along with father, the mother also plays a vital role in a Bodo family. Many works are also done by the Bodo women along with men in a Bodo society. The Bodos are one of the most hardworking tribe. They are always engaged in their domestic works. They plays a significant role in leading their family, weaving traditional attires, plantation and agriculture, cooking, cleaning, welcoming the guests, singing, dancing, worshipping, celebrating festivals, rearing domestic animals and so on. Since time immemorial, the Bodo women also played a role in the protection, promotion and preservation of their culture like language, customary laws, traditional beliefs and so on. For that reason, the Bodo women are considered to be the goddess of wealth in a Bodo family. Even though the Bodo society is patriarchical, the role of Bodo women in a family and society cannot be ignored.

The gender relations of the Bodos which constructs inequality can be analysed looking at the customary law of the community. Customary law is a part of the Bodo traditional customs and practices where the tribe considered it 'intrinsic to their identity and culture'. Customary law can be understood as 'an established system of immemorial rules which evolved from the way of life and natural wants of the people, the general context of which was a common knowledge, coupled with precedents applying to special cases, which were retained in the memories of the chief and his counsellors, their sons and their son's son, until forgotten, or until they became part of the immemorial rules'. The operation of customary laws acts as a powerful tool to define the roles of men and women and dictate acceptable standards of behaviour. Women's social and economic status continues to be influenced by customary rules.

Almost all the customary law of the Bodos which includes 'people's beliefs, customs, social mores, percepts, rites and usages practiced since time immemorial, are not always conducive to the interests of women' and the customary laws relating to 'property and marriage are highly oppressive to women.' As have been mentioned above, women in the region shoulder heavy economic responsibilities viz-a-viz men. Yet their customary laws deny them equal rights to property and inheritence which is one of the important factors affecting the empowerment of the Bodo women.

In most of the Indian families, women do not own property in their own names and donot get share of parental property. Due to weak enforcement of laws protecting them,women continue to have little access to land and property. In fact, some of the lawsdiscriminate against women, when it comes to land and property rights. Though,women have been given rights to inheritance, but the sons had an independent sharein the ancestral property, while the daughter's shares were based on the share receivedby the father. Hence, father could anytime disinherit daughter by renouncing his sharebut the son will continue to have a share in his own right. The married daughtersfacing harassment have no rights in ancestral home.

CHAPTER V

Conclusion

Gender has increasingly been acknowledged as an important variable in analyses and development planning. In recent years, the goals of equality, justice and peace in human development have been adopted by the WID (Women and Development) approach and Sustainable Development Goals which aim to eliminate all forms of discrimination and violence against women in public and private spheres. Gender equality today is not only a fundamental human right but a necessary foundation for a peaceful and sustainable world. Equal access to education, health, decent work, representation in political and economic decision making process are not only rights that women should have ,they also benefit the humanity at large. However, studies reveal that the subject of gender inequality is deep rooted in almost all societies .Women constitute a half of the human race and are subject to discrimination and subordination in the sphere of education, employment, land rights ,food and nutrition etc.

Much academic research on North East India has tended to look at the region as homogenous from the perspective of gender and gender relations, thereby ignoring the diversity in gender related issues. But studies have revealed that women in the North East have been marginalized on various issues of which relations of rights and power have been matters of concern to social scientists. Feminist research have often focused on the need to raise the issue of women's exclusion from the power structure but the fact remains that power is still very much male centric. Even in matrilineal societies like that of the Khasi , Jaintia and Garo, women are excluded from the decision- making process. Besides power relations, other spheres of subordination of women in the North East have been in the area of resource distribution and security over resources like land ,economy, livelihood etc. Literacy and education ,which are the most important indicators of social development also reveal disparity between the sexes. Still another matter of serious concern is the discrimination of women in the economic sector and commodification in the new era of globalization.

It is in this context that the proposed seminar hopes to deliberate on the structure and character of gender disparity in different spheres of social, cultural, economic and political lives of the people of the North-East and thereby try to find a solution to an all-inclusive development of the region.

There are about 190 million adolescents in India- a demographic in which over 30% of people are illiterate. Disparities in gender at this age can often be explained by relatively poor access to reproductive health care and the fact that girls often have less access to food, which adversely affects their growth patterns. Additionally, adolescent girls often work long hours in the home with no opportunity for employment.

Various international gender inequality indices rank India differently on each of these factors, as well as on a composite basis, and these indices are controversial. Gender Inequality in India refers to health, education, economic and political inequalities between men and women. Gender inequalities and their social causes, impact India's sex ratio, women's health over their lifetimes, their educational attainment and economic conditions. Gender

Inequality in India is a multifaceted issue that concerns men and women. Some argue that various gender equality indices place men at a disadvantage. However, when India's population is examined as a whole, women are at a disadvantage in several important ways. In India, discriminatory attitudes towards either sex have existed for generations and affect the lives of both sexes. Although the constitution of India grants men and women equal rights, gender disparities remain.

Research shows gender discrimination mostly in favour of men in many realms including the workplace. Discrimination affects many aspects in the lives of women from career development and progress to mental health disorders. While Indian laws on rape, dowry and adultery have women's safety at heart, these highly discriminatory practices are still taking place at an alarming rate, affecting the lives of many today.

Bibliography:-

Acharya, NN: "A Brief History of Assam" Omsous Publications, New Delhi (2007).

Barpujari, HK: "Political History of Assam" Government of Assam, Calcutta (1977).

Barpujari, HK: "North East India: Politics and Prospects since independence". Spectrum Publications, Guwahati-781001, 1998.

Basumatary, Ionee: "Politics in North East India" Bishal Prakashan, Guwahati-781003 (2014).

Baruah, Sanjib: "India Against Itself, Assam and the politics of Nationality". Oxford University Press, New Delhi-110001, 1999.

Chaudhuri, Kalyan: "New History of Assam and India" Oriental Book Company Private LTD, Guwahati (2004).

Datta, PS: "Autonomy Movement in Assam (Documents)" Omsous Publications, New Delhi-110028, 1993.

Gait, Sir Edward: "A History of Assam" EBH Publishers, Guwahati (2008).

Ghai, KK: "Politics in India" Kalyani Publishers; 1/1, Rajinder Nagar, Ludhiana-141008 (2012).

Goswami, Priyam: "The History of Assam from Yandaboo to Partition, 1826-1947" Orient Black Swan, New Delhi (2012).

Hussain, Monirul: "The Assam Movement, Class, Ideology and Identity" Manak Publication Pvt. Ltd; Delhi-110053, 1993.

JeyasaleenLazamed: "Conflict Mapping and Peace Process in North East India" NESRC, Guwahati (2011).

BIBLIOGRAPHY:-

Kundu, Dilip Kumar: "The State and the Bodo Movement in Assam" A.P.H. Publishing Corporation, New Delhi-11002, 2010.

Pathak, Guptajit: "Politics in India since Independence" Ashok Publication, Panbazar, Guwahati-781003 (2011)

Paul, Dr. Kripesh Chandra: "Politics in India since Independence" ArunPrakashan, Panbazar, Guwahati-781001 (2012).

Prakash, Col Ved: "Encyclopaedia of North East India(Vol 1)" Atlantic Publishers and Distributors(P)LTD; New Delhi (2007).

Prakash, Col Ved: "Encyclopaedia of North East India(Vol 2)" Atlantic Publishers and Distributors(P)LTD; New Delhi (2007).

Prakash, Col Ved: "Encyclopaedia of North East India(Vol 3)" Atlantic Publishers and Distributors(P)LTD; New Delhi (2007).

Prakash, Col Ved: "Encyclopaedia of North East India(Vol 4)" Atlantic Publishers and Distributors(P)LTD; New Delhi (2007).

Prakash, Col Ved: "Encyclopaedia of North East India(Vol 5)" Atlantic Publishers and Distributors(P)LTD; New Delhi (2007).

Thoring, SR: "Violence and Identity in North East India, Naga-Kuki conflict" Mittal Publications, New Delhi (2010).

Rao, V.Venkata; Hazarika, Niru: "A Century of Government and Politics in North East Ind(Vol I); S. Chand and Company LTD; New Delhi (1983).

Rao, V.Venkata; Hazarika, Niru: "A Century of Government and Politics in North East India (Vol II); S. Chand and Company LTD; New Delhi (1983).

BIBLIOGRAPHY:-

Rao, V.Venkata; Hazarika, Niru: "A Century of Government and Politics in North East India (Vol III); S. Chand and Company LTD; New Delhi (1983).

Singh, Chandrika: "North East India: Politics and Insurgency" Manas Publication, Guwahati (2004).

9 798887 723532

Printed by Libri Plureos GmbH in Hamburg, Germany